Breathe

A Reflective Devotional

Jaleesa Cox

Breathe

A Reflective Devotional

Jaleesa Cox

January

January

Week 1
Breathe

Inhale. Exhale. Breathe. This week, I want you to slow
down! Don't worry about your resolutions. "New year,
New me" Don't worry about the when's or the what if's.
Breathe and focus on today. Let tomorrow take care of
itself (Matt 6:33). Now, I'm not saying chuck your goals,
I'm saying don't let them consume you. However, make
sure your goals are God aligned. If they are, then your
desires match His desires and guess what, God gives us
the desires of our hearts (Psalm 37:4 KJV). That means if
your desires are to lose weight or become financially
stable, then, find where His word aligns with your
desires. God wants you healthy and able to pay your light
bill without having to consistently make payment
arrangements. When you find the scripture(s), stand on
it, meditate on it, and tell God you found it (seriously).
Tell him what His word says and that you are expecting it
to come to pass. For example, say God your word
says_____ and I want _____, it aligns
with your word so let it be, because You cannot lie.

Just a Breath

Everyman looks for riches and wealth
Remember life is just a breath

A breath that can be taken and breathed no longer
A breath that can be taken and breathed no longer

Everyman hustles, but only in vain
That's why every man feels so much pain

You cry- Jehovah Shalom, grant me peace, free my mind;
free my heart

My days are numbered and will soon end
My days are numbered and a new life will begin

Jehovah save my soul, oh God save my soul, life isn't
always what it seems

Everyman looks for riches and wealth
Remember life is just a breath

How do you plan to breathe?

January
Week 2
Simply Unwise

Unless the Lord builds the house, they labor in vain that build it; unless the lord guards the city, the watchmen stays awake in vain. Psalms 127:1 NKJV

In my might, I will not try for I will surely fail. For I am sculpted by Your hands and breathe Your breath. Inhale. Exhale. Your hands are mine, my heart is Yours. My natural eyes do not see as my spiritual eyes awaken within me. My foresight is strong. I see sunshine. I see rain, but I see victory all the same. I see Your guidance, as I walk in the steps you pre-set. I run through open doors with thanksgiving. I will not settle for mediocre for you created nothing as such. Continue, I will to drink your Living Water so I am equipped to fight. The battle is not mine but my Lord's. In my might, I will not try for I will surely fail, but with You within me all is well.

Unwise: Trying to do it all by yourself
Wise: Doing all things through Christ who gives you strength (Philippians 4:13)

Unwise: Believing the enemy's, false reports
Wise: Believing what God says. Let God be truth and every other man be a lie (Romans 3:4)

Unwise: Worry
Wise: Taking no thought for tomorrow, resting in His peace (Matthew 6:25)

Side note: Stop trying to do things on your own, invite your Heavenly Father who sits on the throne. For anything you can do with Christ, everything else in simply unwise.

"...For not by my might, nor by power, but by the spirit saith the Lord of host."
 (Zechariah 4:6 KJV)

Bottom Line: unless the Lord leads you, your efforts are in vain

What are you doing that is wise/unwise?

Unwise

_____
_____
_____
_____
_____
_____

Wise

_____
_____
_____
_____
_____
_____

How can you change your unwise decisions to wise decisions?

_____

_____

_____

_____

_____

_____

_____

_____

_____

_____

January
Week 3
How to Create Your World

Change Your Environment

Your environment has a lot to do with who you become. Friends and family are detrimental influences. If your associates seem like they are going nowhere, then you are most likely on a fast path to nowhere. Sit back and look at your environment. Do you see growth? Do you see change for the better? How can you grow? How do you feel after leaving your surroundings? Do you feel uplifted, encouraged, at peace? If your surroundings don't compliment you, change them. For instance, if you wish to be an entrepreneur, then surround yourself with people who have a business mentality. If you wish to be a doctor, are you going to go to law school? I think not!

Mindset Shift

As a man thinks in his heart, so is he (Proverbs 23:7). Basically, saying you are what you think. If you think yourself a failure, then, forget about success. How you truly see yourself is what you will speak aloud, whether positive or negative. Remember words are powerful, they can tear down or build up. The mind is a battleground and you should be on guard daily equipped with the whole armor. Whatever you desire to achieve, believe you can, *say* you can, and stand on His word. Think positively!

Get Out of the Boat

You've changed your environment and shifted your mindset (hopefully), now it's time to get out of the boat and walk on water! Your dreams and ambitions will not fulfill themselves, go for it...I did! Did I always soar, no! I've fallen plenty, at times I felt as if I were barely making it. The key to walking on water is not quitting and staying in faith. When you get out the boat, keep your eyes forward, on the prize, don't look back at the past or the cares of the world around you. Again, keep your eyes on God, don't look at what anyone else is doing because your walk is unique.

Walk on Water

Peter got out of the boat and walked on water,
He took his eyes off the SON and began to falter

He looked at the cares surrounding and became
        Distracted and overwhelmed
He almost arrived unhinged, but lost focus and began to
        Sink but made it in the end.

January
Week 4
Yes

The answer is yes!

Can it be done? Yes! You can do all things with God as your source. You have set goals, maybe created a vision board, which I highly recommend. You need something to see, write the vision down and make it plain. Once you write it down, consult with God about what to pursue first. Then go! (Habakkuk 2:2-3).

Take your time, make sure you revert to Week 1 and breathe, remember life is just a breath! Take one day at a time, don't try to attack everything on your vision board the first week, because you will certainly let yourself down. Spend time with God and take one day at a time. Again, not in your strength but God's. Let the Lord lead you!

February

February
Week 1
Love

For god so loved the world he gave is only begotten son, that whoever believes in him will not perish but have everlasting life. John 3:16 NKJV

God's love covers, God's love cleanses, God's love gives, once pouring from His side, dripping from His body, drenching the earth to cleanse sin...new life begins. Rebirth.

This week I want you to focus on WHY you love the Lord. Specifically, I want you to tell Him all about it. What has He done for you? Has your healing manifested? Did He cheer you up on a dark day? Are you alive? Let Him know.

My Forever Love (My Love Psalm)

You are my forever love, Forever I will praise
You are my forever love who conquered the grave

Every moment with you is different and brand new
It leaves me completely free as I inhale in your hue

Your eyes like fire, burn peace within me
Your touch light, suddenly calms my being

My time with you, I love it as we write our love song

Melodies....the strings play in the background as you make love to me with your words

Promises....you fulfill my desire in its entirety, never faltering on your word

You are my forever love, Forever I will praise
You are my forever love, Sovereign in your reign!

What's your love psalm? Tell Jesus why you love him, tell
him how he makes you feel!

_____

_____

_____

_____

_____

_____

_____

_____

_____

_____

_____

_____

_____

_____

_____

_____

February
Week 2
God is Love

What does blood, water, nails, sacrifice, lashes, and forgiveness have in common? True Love. They all reflect The Cross, Calvary. They were a Choice made by the Father and the Chosen. I see it the John 3:16 way, "For God so Loved the world that he Gave his Only Son, that whoever believes in Him shall not perish but have eternal life." God loved us so much (still does) that He Gave ALL He had for sacrifice. In return, Jesus loved us so much (still does) that He Accepted being a sacrifice so that those who believe in him will live forever through Him and with Him in heaven.

In addition to sacrifice, Jesus forgave, "Father forgive them, for they do not know what they are doing" (Luke 23:34 NIV). In short, He said this while on the Cross before he commanded His spirit to His Father. I thought that was loving of Jesus as He said this after enduring an undeserved punishment of being beaten and mocked before being crucified for the sake of man.

Love

In His love, there is peace and joy. His love is profound and unconditional. His love resembles not of a man and woman, but more like a Father and Son, a crucifixion. There is life and protection. Through His love, one can be comforted, finding peace and acceptance. The love of the Father love is a love like no other; soft, everlasting and never failing. Real. Unconditional.

February
Week 3
Where is my Love?

Your eyes seem hidden, Your voice silent. Where did You go my love? Why are You quiet? I miss the comfort of Your reassurances. I miss the safeness of Your arms. I learn of You through Your word, yet I feel nothing, numbness. Per Your love letter, I won't fight on my own. You said in You I win, but how come I feel defeated? You said give and it shall be given in good measure... yet, I cannot seem to find its treasure.

Despite all, I trust You because I *choose* to. I will be of good courage. Help me along my way oh Lord, help rearrange my life of disarray. Show me the result, my victory through You. Show me your eyes bright like fire flies. Embrace me with the safeness of your arms. Remind me that regardless of the curve balls of life, you cover me, You are Jehovah Rohi, my Shepard and Jehovah Shammah, always there.

What do you do when you feel lost and helpless or forsaken? Choose to TRUST in your Love, Jesus Christ.

February
Week 4
In My Feelings

How do you feel when you think of Jesus? Do you get butterflies? Do you feel a sense of peace?
You are loved by daddy God. Just like any parent, the words "I love you" go a long way. When you wake up, remember to remind God that you love Him. Tell Him how He makes you feel.

...My heart flutters and my soul rejoices for I feel your kiss
Your glory on my tongue, leaves me lost in your midst

-Oh My Soul

March

March
Week 1
Praise Glorious

My worship is real as Your essence amidst my skin. I'm
thankful for the daily breath
I'm given...

This week, I challenge you to worship God in wholeness,
in spirit and in truth (John 4:24). Be real in your worship,
not just words. No lip service, instead, heart service. Put
your heart into it and hear His voice...softer than a
whisper.

Enter worship with thanksgiving and praise, enter
worship with your hands and voice raised. Be genuine.
Place His name in your heart, allow Him full disclosure to
every part. Dance before him like David, sing unto Him a
new psalm.

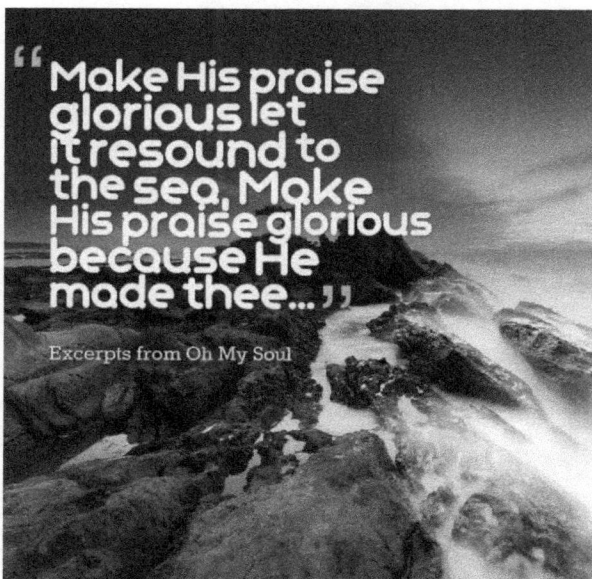

" Make His praise glorious let it resound to the sea, Make His praise glorious because He made thee... "

Excerpts from Oh My Soul

Give God heart service not mouth service. Do your ways give Him praise? If not, how will you change?

_____

_____

_____

_____

_____

_____

_____

March
Week 2
Keep Your Hope On Fire

Get your hopes up today, trust God in every way!

Yes, times will get hard, but keep your hope on fire, for who you hope in is Truth and not a liar. His hope doesn't disappoint while you're perfecting through trials, hold on to His word while going through fire.

My grace is sufficient for you, for my power is made perfect in weakness (2 Corinthians 12:9 NKJV).

But...I felt that God should have _____I felt that he let me down. If you've ever felt that way, tell HIM (He knows anyway!) Say "God I felt you should have _____." After you told him. What did He say? How do you feel now?

Is your Hope still in HIM? Why?

_____

_____

_____

_____

_____

_____

_____

Romans 5:5 NKJV ...now **hope does not disappoint**, because the love of God has been poured out within our hearts through the Holy Spirit who was given to us.

March
Week 3
A Little Longer

After your tears and crying out to God, know that He heard you, your every cry. Wipe your tears and begin to build your faith, for faith moves God, not tears! Yes, He knows you are human, so vent your frustrations away and when you're done, get faithed up! Stand on what God says in His word. Confess it out loud. Every time you begin to feel overwhelmed, confess it. Every time you begin to feel sad, confess it. Every time you being to feel _____ confess it. Confess his word, not what you see!
Confess It!

Confessions:

- [I am superior to my circumstances.] I am more than a conqueror. "Yet in all these things we are more than conquerors through Him who loved us." Romans 8:37 NKJV
- "My God shall supply all my needs according to his riches and glory by Christ Jesus." Philippians 4:19 NKJV
- "The young lions lack and suffer hunger, but those who seek the Lord lack no good thing." Psalms 34:10 NKJV
- "Trust in the Lord with all your heart, and lean not in your own understanding, in all your ways acknowledge him and he shall direct your path." Proverbs 3:5-6 NKJV
- "Therefore do not worry about tomorrow, for tomorrow will worry about its own things. Sufficient for the day is its own trouble." Matthew 6:34 NKJV

- "But seek first the kingdom of God and His righteousness, and all these things will be added to you." Matthew 6:33 NKJV
- "Peace I leave with you; my peace I give you. I do not give as the world gives. Do not let your hearts be troubled and do not be afraid." John 14:27 NIV

"Therefore, I say unto you, take no thought for your life, give all to God and bask in SONlight."

Even though he slay me, yet will I trust him because HIS word cannot lie, by His word I'll abide. I will walk through Shadow's Valley a little longer with no fear because you are with me always and forever.

What are your confessions?

_____

_____

_____

_____

_____

_____

_____

_____

_____

Amen.

March
Week 4
Victory> Defeat

Confession:

I'm superior to my circumstances, as He is so am I. I am superior to my circumstances, He is the word, He cannot lie. No matter what, through wind, rain, or the bliss of sunshine, His love and grace eternally reign which once poured from His side. The defeated foe is currently under my feet, come what may, I shall never retreat. I'm on team victorious for the battle is my Lord's. I'm on team victorious leading with a double-edged sword. I'm superior to my circumstances even when it floods turmoil...Delight I will in Your love in the morning, the words You speak to me are life. Delight I will in Your love at night, as it ends my day quite brightly. Through the wind and rain, it's only for a moment, through the sunshine and pain I'm yet superior to my circumstances as my God Reigns.

Even though it is difficult to view the negative in a positive light, you MUST. When you ignore the negativity, you're not denying it like it's nonexistent. Instead, you're saying whose report you're choosing to believe! Are you going to choose to accept the negative or accept what God says?! Remember WHO you are by remembering WHOSE you are. You are on team victorious, more than a conqueror, and your Father fights your battles (if you let him). Despite the circumstances, make a choice, either life and superiority over adversity or the death of peace and defeat. Regardless of what it looks like, choose to see things God's way. Choose LIFE. Choose Victory. You are SUPERIOR to your circumstances.

#Meaningful Moment

Have faith for Today. Have that Now faith, that Present faith, that unwavering faith, that I believe God no matter what faith!
#havefaith #GrowinHIM

April

April

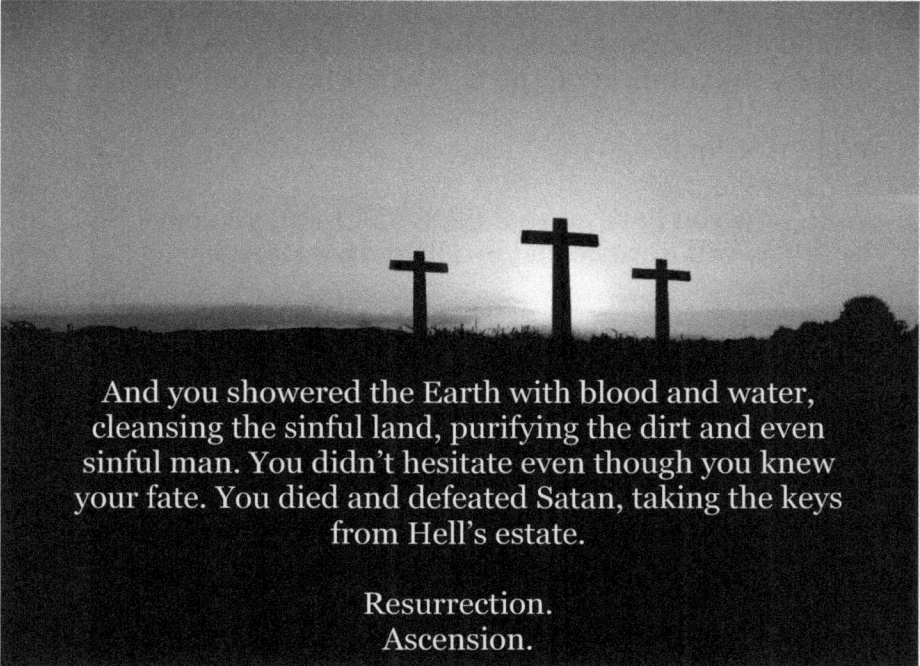

And you showered the Earth with blood and water, cleansing the sinful land, purifying the dirt and even sinful man. You didn't hesitate even though you knew your fate. You died and defeated Satan, taking the keys from Hell's estate.

Resurrection.
Ascension.

April
Week 1
Thankfulness

Yes, I know it's not technically Thanksgiving but we should always give thanks. This week, reflect on the glory of the Cross. Reflect on the freedom it has given you.

What freedom?

Well, now you have eternal life with Christ, you have health as you were healed by His stripes (Isaiah 53:5).

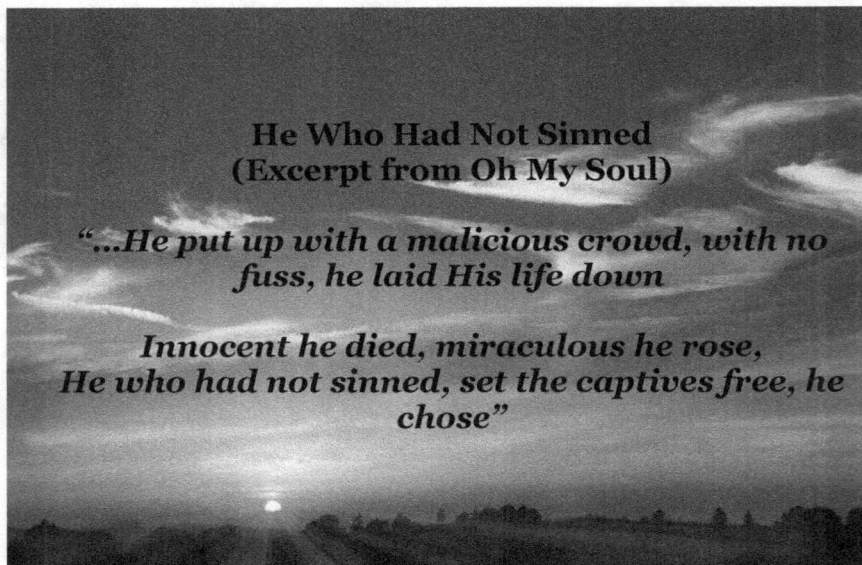

He Who Had Not Sinned
(Excerpt from Oh My Soul)

"...He put up with a malicious crowd, with no fuss, he laid His life down

Innocent he died, miraculous he rose, He who had not sinned, set the captives free, he chose"

April
Week 2
Forgiven

Forgotten is what Jesus is to some of us, His love that was
shed in the form of blood,
Forgotten is His being forsaken, separated from the one
who caressed Him as a child,
What are we to Him? FORGIVEN

You are forgiven. No matter what you have done in the
past, if you have asked for God's forgiveness, He forgave
you and forgot about it. God is the forgiving God. He is
the God of grace and mercy. Grace is what saved
generations on the Cross. Why grace? Well, did the world
deserve a second Adam? No. Grace, God's undeserved
favor gave us Christ. For by grace through faith you are
saved (Ephesians 2:8). With that said, don't think that's a
green light to sin because it's not.

Graciously granted as we were
Redeemed by the blood of the
Anointed one
Crucified on Calvary setting all
Eternally free

April
Week 3
Your May flowers are coming!

You've persisted and stood firm in your faith. By now, you may feel tired, your armor may be a bit torn, needing to be refreshed.

Well, I want to tell you, your 'flowers' are coming! What you've persisted for, stood for in faith, regardless of how it feels, it's coming. God has yet to break a promise, and guess what, He never will. His word is Truth and Life!

"Stand a little longer if you must, In Christ alone, continue to place your trust." -Jaleesa Renee Cox

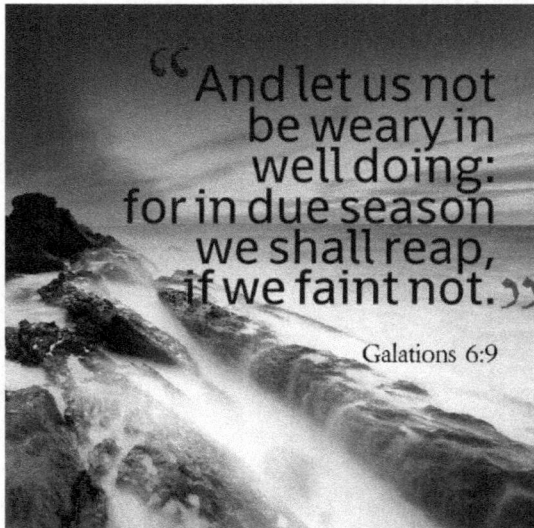

"And let us not be weary in well doing: for in due season we shall reap, if we faint not."

Galations 6:9

April
Week 4
Living Water

I'm deep in this living water, as I delight in your love in the morning which awakens my soul. As I delight in your love, my mind is renewed and my heart cleansed, making my problems grow cold. Your love is as sweet as honey and decadent as chocolate. Your Living Water quenches my soul, seeping into my heart, uttering from my mouth, quenching fiery darts. Your word resembles fire flies dancing in my heart, this love, pure love, I don't want to ever part.

Love poured from Your body and bloodied the earth, seeping inside its cracks as heaven wept... Your Father wept... the angles wept, of Your suffering, of Your demise, of Your death. Your suffering was not in vain, even as Satan indulged in mocking Your temporary captive state.

However, You Lord, had the final word as You defeated Satan in his territory, now everything is under Your feet. Therefore, I will drink of Your Living Water by day and indulge in it by night. I will keep it inside of me so I never lose sight. I will resurrect it in times of trouble, when fiery darts fly my way. I will resurrect it in the noonday, to replenish my soul from a state of dismay. Your Living Water keeps me whole, healthy, and fed. Your Living Water restores all that once was dead. I'm thankful for such a gift, of Your Living Water, I will continue to sip.

He Thought

He thought he won when Adam failed
He thought he won when Jesus was jailed

He thought he won when the Son died upon the Cross
Just to find out, three days later he lost

-Oh My Soul

May

May
Week 1
Though He Slay Me

Though he slay me, yet will I trust him. Job 13:15

Though He slay me, yet will I trust Him. He is the Lord my refuge and strength. He is my solid rock while the earth quakes beneath my feet. He is the One who is the WORD. I will trust him. He is the light within my dark valley, the peace within my storm. I seek Him because HE is. Though He slay me, yet will I trust Him as my victory lies in HIM. Conqueror of Hell and death, bequeathing life and eternal wealth. My cup overflows as His joy strengthens me. Regardless of what life throws my way, regardless of the trials I face. Though He slay me, yet will I trust him.

Will you?

Psalms 23:4 Yea though I walk through the valley of the shadow of death, I will fear no evil; for you are with me; Your rod and Your staff, they comfort me.

Do you allow yourself to be comforted by the King or do you rest in doubt and pity? Do you truly cast your cares or do you pick them back up and caress them for a while? I know it's cliché, but 'let go and let GOD,' when you surrender your worry to Him, really give it to Him, leave it there! I promise you will feel better. Release your burdens, release your pain, rest in the peace Jesus gave.

May
Week 2
Persistence

Persistently pushing through the presence of this life, hoping to one day see the light. It seems as if I live in the trenches. It feels as if I'm forsaken, even though His word states different. I feel alone. I no longer hear the voice of my Love, I no longer feel His touch...

Where are You my love, oh my soul? Why have You left me desolate?
Where are You my love, oh my soul? I'm feeling completely helpless...

I'm tired.

I don't want to be like the Israelites, taking 40 years to complete an 11-day journey (Deut 1:1-3). I don't wish to labor in vain so please build the house my Lord (Psalms 127:1). Persistently, I still push, as my mustard seed faith increased to the size of a pea. I still have more room to grow. The process didn't feel good, however, I'm stronger now. I will continue to persistently push as I rest in my Savior's name.

Side Note: Test and trials don't feel good. Remember, even though you may feel forsaken, you are not. God is with you perfecting you, give Him your all. Diamonds were not always diamonds!

May
Week 3
It's Mine, It's Yours

What exactly is mine or yours? Well, look around. Everything that you see, look at His word, His promises. I recently beheld this revelation. While I was driving on my way to work, I was on 'Pluto' (my day dream place in my head lol) that's when I passed some land (vision minded) and I said "oooh is that mine" and my Heavenly Father said, "it's yours!" I paused, like did I really hear that, and I did. Immediately, when He said "it's yours," here comes the battle of my mind and sultry discouraging voices, that I know are not my Father's.

When HE talks...

See, I'm learning that when you hear God's voice, grab hold to what He says and don't let go...no matter what. Your mind will be the first thing to fight you, well it was for me at least. If that happens, continue to think things pure, holy, good, and true (Philip 4:8). Bury yourself in the word and in praise, feeding your spirit. If those thoughts are resisted, then they *have* to flee. While driving, my mind was attacked. I turned on praise and began to thank the Lord for my land and the vision He has given me, which is certainly bigger than myself but can be accomplished with Him!

Put on and keep on your armor, the armor of God. Even when it feels like you have a break between fights, stay equip, don't let your guard down, that's exactly what the deceiver wants you to do. Instead, stay on guard always. Trials will come to test you. Let them, you will be stronger in the end. I especially had to equip myself because my mind was being attacked from all sides, from doubting what God said to questioning the acquisition of the land.

Rest in His peace. Rest in His assurance that whatever He spoke, IS, even if you don't yet see its manifestation. Stay in faith as His timing is perfect! I have concluded that I can do all with HIM, no matter what. Yes, the vision He's given me is larger than myself (don't you love that!), but I'm not in this alone (neither are you). I shall rest in His peace and follow the steps He ordered. Thank you Lord!

May
Week 4
Rejoice

By looking at the stress of life, I should be overwhelmed. I should seemingly count it all as lost instead of counting it all joy. I should be drowning in despair instead of being of good courage. Besides seeing myself as more than a conqueror, I should look in the mirror and note the failure that I feel l like...I mean, things that should of went right, went so far left. It's like I'm being fought constantly in my mind. Thoughts ranging from God's ability, the power in His word, to wondering if it was His voice I heard.

Make a Choice

What will I decide? Will I decide to count it all joy? Will I decide that I am more than a conqueror? Will I decide to be of good courage? Yes! If I am going to fight, it's going to be a good one, one that I win because my God is able and He is victorious. See, I've been from unemployed, in a car accident, and everything in between. The fire of the fight is serious, it's hard, it's refining. I've felt refined on many occasions. However, through it all, I've never stopped bearing fruit, Amen. Jeremiah 17:7-8 NKJV reads, "Blessed is the man who trusts in the Lord, and whose hope is in the Lord. For he shall be like a tree planted by the waters, which spreads out its roots by the river, and will not fear when heat comes; but its leaf will be green, and will not be anxious in the year of drought, nor will cease from yielding fruit." See, amid what appeared to be my worse, I was/am blessed because I chose to put my trust in the Lord, regardless of circumstance. I also didn't stop yielding fruit, I had

42

everything I needed and desired and it was a bonus that items on my vision board were/are constantly being filled. God is true to his word. He has no choice or be deemed a liar. Believe it!

What choice will you make? Why?

_____

_____

_____

_____

_____

_____

_____

_____

_____

_____

Now that you've made a choice, hold on to it, nurture it with the Word.

Free

With your loving arms around me, I feel safe
With your arms, you comfort me
All my troubles and pains flee, I become loose, I become
      free

All my strongholds, all my cares, disappear in the light of
      your presence
I become strong, embraced with your love, thankful for
      the taste of your essence

With your loving arms, the weight of the world doesn't
      bother me
I feel free, blessed indeed, and thankful that you
      surround me

My burdens are immediately lifted, my spirit breathes
My pains are transcended, my soul sings

All my walls become grounded, you bless me indeed
You elevate me from my pit, I am immediately freed

-Oh My Soul

June

June
Week 1
Be Still

This peace, the feeling I've longed for...

We hustle and bustle on our daily grind, make sure you take time to rest, unwind. As you rest, be still and know that God is in the utmost control.

Confession: Today, I choose to rest in the comfort of Your word. I'm giving You all my cares and I'm going to leave them there. I'm no longer concerned.

1 Peter 5:7 NASB casting **all** your anxiety on Him, because He **cares** for you.

What are you surrendering to Jesus?

_____

_____

_____

_____

_____

_____

_____

_____

_____

_____

Amen.

June
Week 2
#Slow Down

Relax, take a breath, don't doubt, don't worry, in the end it will all work out keep going. Shout with a voice of triumph, praise His name on High, for your love is the God of the sky. He hears. He listens. He provides. He loves. He Is. Don't worry about tomorrow all your needs are supplied, believe it, receive it with His word free of lies
(Matthew 6:33).

It's the middle of the year...breathe. Everything is handled because God's got you. Slow down and relax. Rest in His peace.

Remember He is God! #rest #bestill #breathe

How will you rest today?

_____

_____

_____

_____

_____

_____

_____

_____

_____

June
Week 3
Impossibly Possible

"...All things are possible to he who believes." (Mark 9:23 NKJV)

Yes, that's right even through impossible looking situations, give it to God, listen to Him and watch Him move mountains for you. He knows all, seek His wisdom, have the mind of Christ. Speak truth, and watch the impossible come to life. God making the impossible possible, speaking creation into existence from day one, Christ making the impossible conceivable as victory is present before the battle begun. Believe it, receive it you shall have what you say, for the heart speaks what you believe so believe *life* today.

What are some impossible looking situations you are faced with?

_____

_____

_____

_____

_____

_____

_____

_____

_____

_____

What does God's Word say? Now...meditate on His word.

June
Week 4
Be Content

Are you content with your season? Are you able to handle what's currently on your plate? If you are unable to answer, then, you may need to work on being content in your season.

Contentment

As humans, we always want more. We don't want to start small, we desire to go big. Well, the bible says don't despise small beginnings (Zechariah 4:10), whether in ministry, business, or anything else you do, its ok to start small. When God sees you are able to steward a little, then He can gradually increase you. As the loving father He is, He's not going to give you more than you can handle. He desires the best for you and His timing is *everything*. Know that God wants to increase all areas of your life, from health to wealth. He is a good father. He is the giving God. Be content because God is not...He wants to grow you.

Trust

Trust in the Lord with all your heart, And lean not on **your** own understanding; **In all your** ways acknowledge Him, And He shall direct **your** paths.
Proverbs 3:5-6 NKJV

One way of being content is trusting God. Do you trust God to elevate you? Do you trust Him to complete what He has promised? Do you believe that His timing is best? If not, begin digging into the word. When you feel a sense of worry or fear, fight it with the word, "God hath not given me a spirit of fear; but a spirit of power, love, and of a sound mind" (2 Timothy 1:7KJV). "My soul wait silently from God alone, my expectation is from him" (Psalm 62:5 NKJV). Whenever you begin to feel like you are losing joy, go to the Word, its Living Water. Drink and be well.

"...**Man shall not live by bread alone**, but by every word that proceeds from the mouth of God.'" Matthew 4:4 NKJV

#Meaningful Moment

No matter what you are facing remember it is through HIM you remain strong and through HIM there's victory. Keep walking, keep fighting, and keep your faith. You got this! Why? Because God's got you!

> "In *Christ* alone,
> I stand *strong*
> as waves crash
> around me,
> *thankful* for His
> *blood*, His *victory*
> surrounding"
>
> @jaleecox

July

July

You are a breathtakingly beautiful concoction of my sin. You spoke quite beautifully as the walls caved in. Your words entice sultry promises. Your words are full of lies, yet they pull me in deeper with their captivating lights. The lights of your words cascade around my mind and penetrate my heart. I must stop this, I must fight for the truth is freeing. The truth is the I AM, redeeming. I must stop this before my light turns to darkness, my flame extinguished...Breathtakingly beautiful concoction of my sin, you are no longer welcome here again.

July
Week 1
Die Another Way

Don't feed it, starve it, let it die. Allow your spirit man to rise. Be the mighty warrior you are in Christ, take ye the land and conquer it as Love conquered the grave.

Jesus is the only living water, drink and be well.

We must refresh ourselves daily with the Living Water of Christ; replenishing our armor, building our faith, keeping our inner man strong...as whatever is fed grows stronger.

How? Stay in God's word and meditate on it daily, let it slip into your inner man. When troubled times arise, say what thus saith the Lord. When you do this, you build your faith.

Feed your faith, not fear. Just as God needs mustard seed faith, Satan needs mustard seed fear. When he sees your fear, he will do everything he can to magnify your situation. Remember, regardless of circumstance, turn to God's word, let it arise from your heart and speak it from your mouth. #DeathtoFlesh

Forever
Leading to death versus
Eternal life, temporally
Satisfying as a seductive torment to
Hell

How are you going to die another way?

It doesn't feel good but it is completely worth it.

July
Week 2
Fetal Position

Today, I feel like fighting! Our fights are not of this world but of flesh and blood, principalities and powers. We fight in spirit. During trying times, keep your spirit fed so you will have something to fight with. Keep your mouth pure, for what we speak, manifests. Your words are like seeds that penetrate the ground. If constantly watered, it shall sprout, whether good seed or bad seed. Stand, as you are waiting for your suddenly, your breakthrough, the manifestation of your prayers. Stand. Stand in prayer, stand in thanksgiving. Live what you are praying for has already manifested. When the deceiver throws his weapons in attempts to discourage you, stand. Hold on to the Word, put your battledress on and scream Battle Cry!

Fetal Position

I will Not stand down, I will fight 'till the end
I will Not give up, I will Not give in

I will not allow problems to be the last of me
I will not allow hurt to destroy me

Opposition I may encounter, but it can't have me
The deceiver's devices will not penetrate my being

For my shield is held high and my battle dress on
My sword is sharp, I can fight no matter for how long

He will not see me weak, he will not see me cry,
He will not see me broken, he can try and try

I choose to not let him laugh in my face

I choose to make him the mockery, a disgrace

I choose to fight
I choose to win

Jab left, Jab right, black eye to my opposition
Jab right, uppercut, left, knock out... I won, opposition's
in a fetal position!!

What are you doing to ensure your opposition is in a fetal position? Are you giving it completely to God? Are you refreshing yourself with the Living water daily? What are you doing?

_____

_____

_____

_____

_____

_____

_____

_____

_____

_____

Hello Victorious!

July
Week 3
Like a Lion

He stalks his pray, looking for the weak, keep your armor on, in your flesh don't think.

Stay well equipped with the sword of the spirit, slice his deceitful words to millions of pieces. Don't let him see you sweat for he is surely coming. Don't run, scream battle cry, for you are victorious, triumphant. Hold your ground, don't turn your back, guard your heart and mind, keep your eyes on track, view things pure. Give the adversary no authority...he stalks his prey like a roaring lion, keep your armor on and don't relent, for victory through Christ is already given.

1Peter 5:9

July
Week 4
Jubilee

Stand fast therefore in the liberty by which Christ has made us free, and do not be entangled again with a yoke of bondage. Galatians 5:1 NKJV

True freedom is Christ. Christ set you free from the world as you are in the world but not of the world. Regardless of what happens in life, regardless of the principalities you fight, you are free. Rest in Christ, sip from His Living Water. You became free on the Cross. But He *was* **wounded for our transgressions**, *He was* bruised **for our** iniquities; the chastisement for our peace *was* upon Him, and by His stripes we are healed (Isaiah 53:5 NKJV). At that moment, you became free, whole, and complete. You crossed over from dark/death to light/life. You have a healed life. You have eternal life. Amen.

Whenever you begin to feel overwhelmed, don't! Refresh yourself with the Living Water, remind yourself of your freedom that was bought with a price. Revert to the word of God. If you have a gloomy doctor's report, revert to the word and remind yourself Jesus paid it, more month than money, Jesus paid it, need grace and mercy, Jesus paid it. Whatever you think you might lack, Jesus paid it. Be Free!

Jesus paid it!

How are you going to rest in the freedom of Christ?

_____

_____

_____

_____

_____

_____

_____

_____

_____

_____

_____

_____

August

August
Week 1
Listen Up!

Sometimes you want your love to come quickly because you're feeling lost or alone. Well there's good news, you're not alone. His word says He is Jehovah Shammah, "...the Lord is there" (Ezekiel 48:35). He is always with you even when you feel alone or forsaken no matter what.

When you begin to feel forsaken, rest and be still. You need to do this so you can hear His voice and experience the calmness of His presence. Most likely, without realization, you are letting the loudness of your mind (thoughts that are not of God) and the busyness of life (cares of this world) consume you. In that instance, you need to slow down and make time to relax and rest in God. One moment with God can erase the feeling of loneliness and demolish burdens. Life throws curveballs, it's up to you to decide how to handle them. Get those ants out your pants and heed voice of the glorious one!

How will you listen? I will listen by

_____
_____
_____
_____
_____
_____
_____
_____
_____
_____
_____
_____

"Acknowledge God while in your pain, proclaim His word aloud and watch His power bring change. "-Jaleesa Renee Cox

August
Week 2
Whisper in My Ear

His words are softly spoken, softer than a whisper. Be
still or you'll regretfully miss it.

Whisper in my Ear

Sitting here, I see what has become, hoping, praying that
        circumstances change
Sitting here, wondering will this always be, and hoping to
        find freedom amongst misery

My chains are thick and seem impossible to break
I'm bound, my strength has left me, and my life is at steak

I cry out, but a reply I hear not
My eyes begin to stream, I feel forgotten

I have dark days and sleepless nights
My eyes have no use for I am blind

I cry out once more, and the wind spoke
At once I felt relieved, I felt freed

My chains disintegrated, my body strengthen, my eyes
        open, I now have peace
I cried out, you answered in the wind, a whisper in my ear

When did God whisper in your ear? What did He say?

_____

_____

_____

_____

_____

_____

_____

_____

_____

_____

_____

_____

...take Him at His word today.

August
Week 3
Wisdom Please!

If any of you lack wisdom, let him ask of God, that giveth
to all men liberally, and upbraideth not; and it shall be
given him. James 1:5 KJV

Today Lord, my Father God, I need your wisdom in my
life.

One way to receive God's wisdom is to ask Him (James
1:5). God also gives us the desires of our hearts. (Psalms
37:4) If you desire His wisdom in your life, why wouldn't
He give it to you?

Another way is to examine your environment, meaning
the people in your surroundings. Proverbs 13:20 NASB
reads "He who walks with wise men will be wise, But the
companion of fools will suffer harm." Your surroundings
are crucial to your growth or lack thereof. Surround
yourself with vision minded people, Jesus minded people.
Make sure they bear fruit, as a tree is known by its fruit.
By fruit, I don't only mean materials like finances, but
also peace, joy, loving others, and patience etc.

Luke 6:43-45 KJV
"For a good tree bringeth not forth corrupt fruit; neither
doth a corrupt tree bring forth good fruit. For every tree is
known by his own fruit. For of thorns men do not gather
figs, nor of a bramble bush gather they grapes. A good
man out of the good treasure of his heart bringeth forth
that which is good; and an evil man out of the evil
treasure of his heart bringeth forth that which is evil: for
of the abundance of the heart his mouth speaketh."

Think about it! Who are you walking with? How does their fruit look on you? Do you like what you see spiritually?

If you don't like what you see, how are you going to change it?

_____

_____

_____

_____

_____

_____

_____

_____

_____

_____

_____

_____

_____

August
Week 4
Who are You Seeking?

What are you seeking? Are you seeking validation in a job, friendship, or another human? Are you seeking things, material STUFF because you need it (or so you think)?

If you are seeking material things or the provision of your needs, please stop and revert to Matthew 6:33 KJV "But **seek** ye **first the kingdom** of God, and his righteousness; and all these things shall be added unto you." God, your heavenly father knows you live in a world that runs on money! He knows you have car notes, light bills, and the latter, so seek Him. He has not changed. He is the same God that fed Elijah by a raven! (1Kings 17:4; 6) He will feed you too! #wonthedoit #yesHewill #sameGOD

Looking for validation much? Stop. You are 1Peter 2:9 status "But ye are a chosen generation, a royal priesthood, a holy nation, a peculiar people; that ye should shew forth the praises of him who hath called you out of darkness into his marvellous light" You are chosen, peculiar, you are meant to stand out of the crowd, not blend in. You are born to stand out for Christ. Embrace it. Embrace Him. Live unashamed for God as he died unashamed for you.

Live unashamed for God as He died unashamed for you.

71

September

September
Week 1
Where Art Thou?

I've looked my eyes to the hills, where is my help? It seems hidden behind the midsummer night clouds. How did I get here...happenstance?

How do I find my help when it seems hidden?

1. Be persistent. Keep searching because help is present, keep your eyes raised high, while you're in your fight scream battle cry. We fight the good fight, the fight of faith, stay persistent and finish your race as you are covered in God's grace.

2. Keep Faith Alive. Don't relinquish your faith, don't quit. Continue believing in His word given. Speak His word, confess it and nothing else. Remember your tongue holds the power of life and death.

Help Where Art Thou?

What should I do when I feel such a way? I know, its cliché but I should praise!

Why are you downcast, Oh My Soul, why are you depressed within me?
Why do you lament when you belong to the King of Victory?

Raise your head to the Hills and praise until you see sunshine
Raise your praise aloud, scream battle cry

Help is here, help is now, believe in God's word, receive it now

Proverbs 18:21 Death and life are in the power of your tongue.

Remember, Jesus didn't do or say anything unless He heard or saw the Father do it (John 5:19).

How are you going to use your words?

_____

_____

_____

_____

_____

_____

_____

_____

_____

_____

_____

_____

_____

_____

September
Week 2
Same God

As the seasons change, God remains the same! He is the same God that parted the Red Sea, the same God who rose His SON to victory. His power is unending, unimaginable. He is the Change you need in your life. Change into His way of doing things instead of attempting things out of your own strength. Look in the Word, and see what He has already done, see how He delivered, see that He has healed. Once you see that He is the same God as before, believe that He can and will demonstrate His miraculous power in your life.

When things seem to constantly not work, *YOU* may be trying to accomplish it in *YOUR* strength. Did Peter heal the beggar at the gate called Beautiful or did he let the Power of God work through him to heal the beggar (Acts3)? Did Peter's shadow heal people (Acts 5:14-16) as he walked by, or was it God through him, as Peter was but a man? If Peter or anyone tried to accomplish healing the sick or raising the dead, in their strength, they would have failed.

Matthew 16:26 KJV
"But Jesus beheld them, and said unto them, With men this is impossible; but with God all things are possible."

September

Week 3
Who's in Your Corner?

Who's in your corner, by your side, who goes before you to calm the tide? Who fights your battles so they end in victory, who speaks truth and says taste and see? Who has healed every sickness known to man, who has provided everything in abundance to man? Who is He? He is The I AM, The Lord God Almighty, The King of Glory.

Who is HE to you?

_____

_____

_____

_____

_____

_____

_____

_____

Sometimes, we as flawed humans get caught up in ourselves. For example, how are we going to manifest something or how we are going to get healed? Now, that is not to say don't listen to the doctor, I'm saying whose report are you going to believe?! If the doctor says don't intake too much sugar and you overindulge daily, of course there will be consequences, a larger waist line and maybe diabetes. If that happens, remind yourself who's in your corner. Take the necessary steps to reduce sugar intake, while reminding yourself you can do all things. Give God something to work with, ask Him for help!

As a father, God wants to help you. How are you going to use who's in your corner?

_____

_____

_____

_____

_____

_____

_____

_____

_____

September

Week 4
Smile

She is more precious than rubies, and all the things you may desire cannot compare with her. Proverbs 3:15 NKJV

Hello beautiful, how are you, you lovely jewel to be adorned? I hope you are resting in the presence of the King, allowing Him to comfort you from everything. Hello beautiful and wonderfully made, I hope the Son shines your way. I hope you realize and know your worth, you are beautifully created in the image of God. No matter what society may say, please see yourself God's way! You are sunshine, you are Queens, and you are God's walking masterpiece. Your eyes, your lips, your skin, your hips. Every curve, every roll, tall or short, you are worth more than gold. Hello beautiful.

#Meaningful Moment

Holdfast and stand strong, continue to place your trust in the Holy One. #alittlelonger #juststand

Stand a little longer if you must, In Christ alone, continue to place your trust.

saymysoul.com

October

October
Week 1
Cemented Feet

My back seemingly against the wall as what appears to be reality caving in. My thoughts race, my mind wonders, but I must control this feeling. I mustn't let it consume me and seep inside my heart, for it truly will sprout. I must fight with all that's within me to prevent from a dreadful loss. Even though things seem gloomy and a bit dismay, I will forever praise You for You are faithful every day. My shoulders seem weighted down. I feel as I can barely walk, my feet feel as if they trudge through cement...unmoving. It feels as if I am going nowhere fast, like I'm vacationing in a desert...always thirsty, always in need.

However, Your grace *carried* me. Your grace *carries* me.

You lift my feet so they move. Surround me You do with Your love and guidance, never allowing me to take on more than I can handle. You will always see me through (1 Cor 10:13). Step one, step two. I'm closer to my manifested victory. The air is getting clearer, my cemented feet are beginning to fragment. Step three, step four, I feel more of Your grace that carries me. My steps begin to quicken as I begin to increase my pace. The cement on my feet has crumbled and I am completely freed. I run in the delight of my lover, my friend, my Grace. As in You I am a victor, a conqueror. In You, I defeat the evils that revolt against me forming weapons that shall not prosper. In you I can do all things (Phil 4:13). I am forever thankful.

Forever tried and true the
All seeing sufficient one, forever
I will praise you, my love, oh my soul
Thankful for your grace covering my steps and your
Heartbeat that dances united within me
Fulfilling my every desire with
Unlimited overflow, thank you for your
Loyalty and grace, thank you my Faithful forever love

October
Week 2
The One Surrounding

Tying to not be overcome by the cares of this world.
Trying not to feel dismay. Trying not to look at my
surroundings, instead look at The ONE surrounding. This
is hard, as I feel as if I'm going through Hell. My faith
seems to be on trial, however my trust is in You. I will not
falter, I will not faint, and I will forever bask in the
presence of Your grace. I will get drunk on Your Living
Water, until my cup overflows. I refuse to listen to the
voices in my head. I refuse to allow them to seep inside
my heart. I will be ok as I am more than a conqueror. As
Samuel Rodriguez says, "I am who the I AM says I am."

I am
- more than a conqueror
- the head and not the tail
- victorious
- followed by goodness and mercy all my days
- determined
- loved

...simply unbothered. I will not succumb to my thoughts.
I will bask in Your grace. My battledress is on, the shield
in guard of my face. Weapons will form, but they have
nowhere to go. They will not prosper because my God
won't allow them to.

Who are you?

_____

_____

_____

_____

_____

_____

_____

_____

_____

_____

_____

_____

_____

_____

_____

Now **act** like it!

October

Reflect the past, what didn't work, place your energy on the now, speak positive words. Renew yourself in the word of God, rest in His promises, trust in His word. God comforts, God cares, His love is everlasting, and it never fails.

Today: This is the day the Lord has made; I will rejoice and be glad in it (Psalms 118:24).

This day, choose to rejoice. This day, choose to leave the past in the past. This day, choose life to your situation. This day, choose to be free, choose to fully trust in God's word and rest in His promises. Some of His many promises are included in Psalms 103:1-8.

1. He promises our **forgiveness of all our sins**. He is the forgiving God.
2. **Healing all our diseases**. He is the healing God.
3. **Redeeming your life from destructions**. He is the redeeming God.
4. You are **crowned with loving-kindness** and tender mercies. He is love and mercy.
5. **You are satisfied**. He satisfies your mouth with good things so your youth is renewed like the eagles,
6. **You are free** from oppression. He breaks chains!
7. Makes his way known to you. **He leads and guides** you like the good Shepard he is.
8. **Gives you grace and mercy** in your time of need. He is always there to help.

Note: You're only supposed to reflect on the past, not build a house and stay there. For instance, if you tried to do things in your strength and it didn't work, then, remember it and don't make the same mistake.

October

Week 4
If He Is, Then Who Am I?

If He is, then who am I? Well first, establish who He is. Who is God to you? Is He a lecturer, a friend, a healer etc.? If you don't know who He is to you, then you will never experience His power of that area. For instance, if you don't know God as the healer and you don't believe He has healed you while on Calvary, then you will never experience the manifestation of His healing power. To me, like salvation, if you believe you are saved then you are. Do you see your salvation happening, not likely. However, you just know it and in some cases and feel His presence! Whatever you believe, so be it.

If Jesus is your healer, call yourself healed. If Jesus is your provider, call yourself cared for. If Jesus is your love, call yourself loved. If He is your light, then you no longer dwell in darkness. Amen.

If He is, then who are you?

_____

_____

_____

_____

_____

_____

November

November

Week 1
O give thanks of he is good... Ps 136:1

You breathe, you live, you hustle for a buck, don't forget to fulfil your purpose before time is up. Every man looks for riches and wealth, remember life is just a breath. Inhale. Exhale.

Have you thanked the Lord lately? Not just in passing, but told Him how and why you are thankful. I've come to the realization that God loves thanksgiving just as much as He loves our praise. Thank God for everything. Thank Him for breath. Thank Him for provision. Thank Him for His love and faithfulness and favor. Give thanks for every good thing that happens, as every good thing is from Him (James 1:17). It can take the form of something small as a close parking spot to a bill being paid.
Thank Him in the morning, thank Him in the noonday. Thank Him at night, for God loves you forever, and is always by your side.

What are you thankful for...really?
1.

_____

_____

_____

2.

_____

_____

_____

3.

4.

5.

November
Week 2
Why so Thankful?

Today I show gratitude for what You have already done, sending Your only begotten, the once forsaken SON. The earth drank from His body as His blood purified the earth and man, cleansing every crevasse that every heart wills.

My God is an awesome God. Glory to the Father for sending His Son. Glory to the Son who accepted His fate. Thank you oh my King. By now, you have recorded what you are thankful for. Now, revisit your thankful top five and write *why* you are thankful.

Why are you thankful for those things/people?

1.

_____

_____

_____

2.

_____

_____

_____

3.

_____

_____

_____

4.

5.

November
Week 3
PDA of Thanks

Don't talk about it, be about it! By now, you have stated your thankful top 5. Now, let's be about it. It's time to show your gratitude. Think of one gesture you could do to display your appreciation. For instance, a card, a video message, praising God just because, doing the dishes etc. How are you going to show your gratitude? Dig deep and put some thought into it.

I will show my gratitude by...
1.

2.

3.

4.

5.

November
Week 4
Praise is Necessary

Confuse the enemy with your praise radically, fervently with voices raised. The thief attacks in 3 ways as he comes to steal, kill, and destroy (John 10:10). He wants to steal your joy. He will try to take it through any way, something as small as a flat tire or thinking people are talking about you (because they have nothing better to do, right?!). The enemy wants your peace, your life. Don't let it happen. When you feel your joy or peace slipping, bring on the praise. It's cliché, but praise does confuse the enemy. When the enemy thinks he fired his best shot to take you out, and instead you elevate in praise, you call him defeated to his face!

List 3 reasons why You praise.

1.

_____

_____

_____

2.

_____

_____

_____

3.

_____

_____

_____

"When the enemy thinks he fired his best shot to take you out, and instead you elevate in praise, you call him defeated to his face!" -Jaleesa Renee Cox

#Meaningful Moment

Jesus is the Reason. Halleluiah the Birth of the King!
#Hecame #Hegave #Helives

December

December
Week 1
The Month of Giving

As family and friends gather around, let's not forget the reason Grace abounds!

The holidays are a joyous time where families come together, let's not get wrapped up into the earthly treasure. Christ came, died, and resurrected so we can live forever. This holiday season and every day, I challenge you to give. Give the gift of the fruits of the spirit.

Give love even to those who seem undeserving as Christ bled for them too. **Give joy.** How? A smile will do. You never know, you may be the only one who acknowledges their presence. **Give peace.** Be available to listen to someone's pain, then turn them to the Prince of Peace. Remind them they were bought with a price, and guess what, peace came with it!

How will you give this week? "...you shall love your neighbor as yourself." Matthew 22:39 NKJV

I will give love by...

_____

_____

_____

"The joy of the Lord is my strength." Nehemiah 8:10
I will give joy by...

_____

_____

_____

_____

"Depart from evil and do good; seek peace and pursue it."
Psalms 34:14 NKJV
I will give peace by...

_____

_____

_____

_____

Luke 6:38 NIV "Give, and it will be given to you. A good
measure, pressed down, shaken together and running
over, will be poured into your lap. For with the measure
you use, it will be measured to you."

December
Week 2
Endure

"Love is patient, love is kind..." (1 Corinthians 13:4). **Be patient.** When interacting with friends and family who seem to constantly backslide, try to understand their view point. I'm not saying agree with them, but if they are willing, guide them using the wisdom of God. Don't discard them no matter how many times they fall. I'm not saying be a crutch, but have an open heart to listen. Encourage them, remind them who they are in Christ. A righteous man may fall seven times, but gets back up eight (Proverbs 24:16). Think. How would you want God to treat you if the roles were reversed?

Also, be patient not only with people, but also with God. You've planted seeds, some spiritually and some financially. Well, seeds take time to grow! While you are waiting, God is perfecting you. What's the use of getting a harvest you are not mature enough to handle? You will most likely lose it and it will destroy you, just like the prodigal son who took his inheritance and wasted it (Luke 15). God's timing is perfect anyway.

Wait on the Lord; be of good courage, and he shall strengthen your heart; wait, I say, on the Lord.
Psalms 27:14 NKJV

I will be patient with God by...

_____

_____

_____

_____

I will be patient with family and friends by...

December
Week 3
Be Kind

Be kind. Kind gestures go a long way. From a smile, to holding the door for the person after you, or paying for the following car in the drive thru. In this respect, you are doing unto others as you would like them to do unto you (Luke 6:31). Think about it, it goes back to sowing and reaping. Whatever you put in the ground you will eventually receive. For example, if you sow kindness, you will reap kindness. You may reap it through gesture, someone allowing you to go before them at checkout, anything. That's kindness. Likewise, if you sow bad seeds or treat people in an ungodly way, then, you will reap a harvest as such.

How will you sow kindness?

_____

_____

_____

_____

_____

_____

December
Week 4
Who am I? I AM the Way!

I am the way, the truth, the life, no one cometh to the Father except by me John 14:6 KJV.

Rejoice and be glad that the Way came. He came, born in a manger, swaddled in clothes, in the lowest predicament, but He rose in fame. When He walked, when He talked, He only reciprocated the Father. He is the I AM. He journeyed from carpenter to Savior, suffering for the undeserving. His blood poured from His back, filling the earth's cracks. Cleansed.

You are pure, you are righteous because of the Price He paid. He sits at the right hand of God the Father, in constant intercession. He's omnipresent. The Way came, died, and Lives. The Way is Jesus who still IS!

Remember in everything, Jesus is the Way!

Let's Connect!

Facebook: Say My Soul

Instagram: @saymysoul or @jaleecox

Twitter: @jaleecox

Email: info@saymysoul.com

Websites: saymysoul.com and jaleesacox.com

www.ingramcontent.com/pod-product-compliance
Lightning Source LLC
Chambersburg PA
CBHW031520040426
42445CB00009B/318